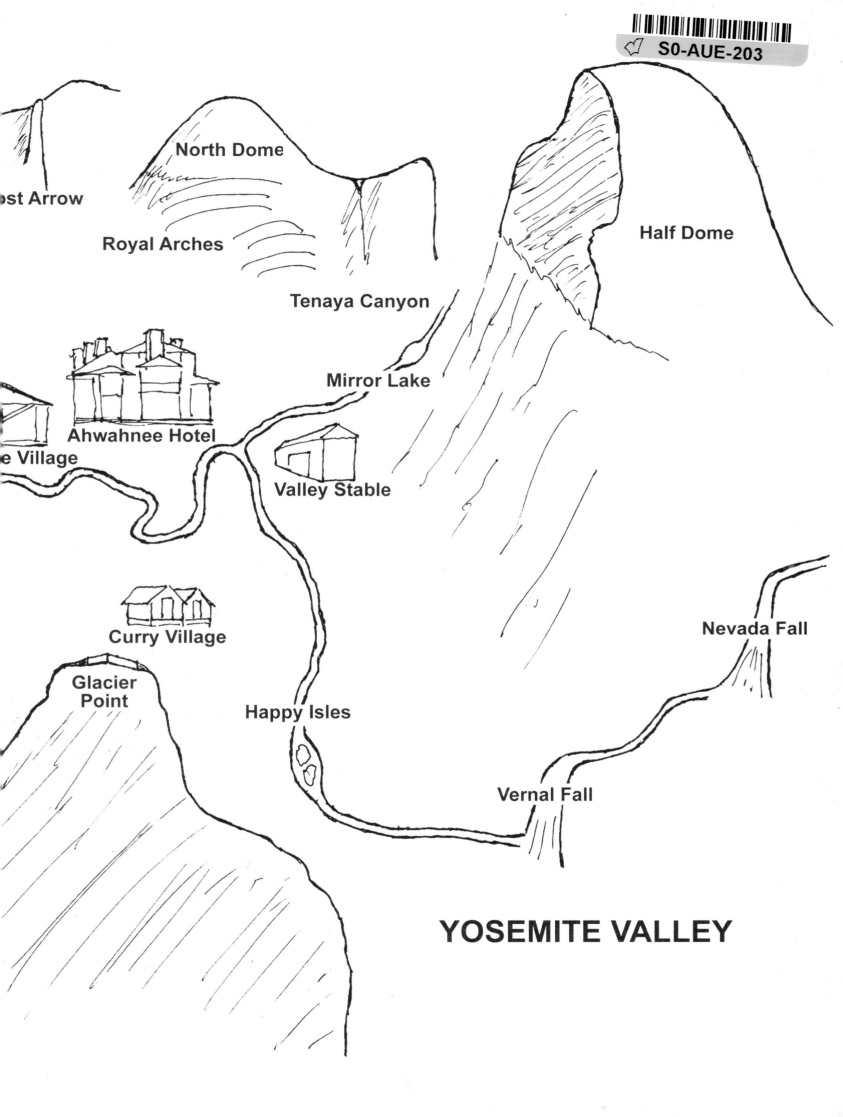

THIS IS
YOSEMITE VALLEY

An Introduction to Yosemite National Park

by J. Richard Gaskill
with drawings by Tim Kain

ഇൽ

TO CHERIE
Dick Gaskill
04/08

PARK PLACE PUBLICATIONS
PACIFIC GROVE, CALIFORNIA

THIS IS YOSEMITE VALLEY
An Introduction to Yosemite National Park

Text and photographs by J. Richard Gaskill with drawings by Tim Kain

ISBN 978-1-877809-49-1

Printed in China

First U.S. Edition: October 2007

Published by Park Place Publications, Pacific Grove, California

www.parkplacepublications.com

Dedication

To my daughters, Jackie, Andrea, and Katie,
who endured many trips to Yosemite in their younger
years—hiking, backpacking, skiing, climbing, and
even snow-camping ...

... and to some special Yosemite people: Bill Russell,
Sheridan King, Renate Binder, and Karin Prichard,
whose advice and guidance on adventures ranging
from day-hiking, to climbing, to back-country
exploration have been invaluable over the years.

Author

Dick Gaskill, a retired physician, lives in Los Gatos,
California, in the greater San Francisco Bay Area. Over
the past 40 years he has spent many days and weeks in
Yosemite with family and friends—hiking, backpacking,
skiing, climbing, and snow-camping—always with a
camera. He and his wife, Kathleen, were recently
married at the Ahwahnee Hotel.

Graphic Artist

Tim Kain, a contemporary of Gaskill's daughters and
long-time family friend, is an accomplished graphic
artist. He is very familiar with Yosemite, and also lives
in Los Gatos with his wife, Lucy, and their two sons.

෴

THIS IS YOSEMITE VALLEY

AN INTRODUCTION TO YOSEMITE NATIONAL PARK

This is an introduction to Yosemite for the family.
It is about how this beautiful place came to be,
geologically and politically, and what to see and do.

The focus is on the natural features in Yosemite Valley,
the most spectacular part of the park
and the destination of most visitors.

Readers of all ages will appreciate
the concise descriptions, and will immediately
recognize the spires, domes, waterfalls,
and big walls when they visit.

ഓരു

CONTENTS

ℐ℔ℛ

Welcome to Yosemite

There are three entrance stations on the west side of Yosemite which provide easy access to the valley. The fourth entrance, to the east, is about two hours from the valley and is closed during the winter.

THIS IS YOSEMITE VALLEY

Yosemite Valley is a tiny part of Yosemite National Park. At an elevation of 4000 feet, it is seven miles long, less than a mile wide, and surrounded by 3000-foot granite walls.

EL CAPITAN

HALF DOME

It is one of the most unique and beautiful places on Earth, with spires, domes, and waterfalls along the rim; and meadows, streams, and forest on the floor. Don't miss this view point, just west of Bridalveil Fall on Hwy 41.

BRIDALVEIL FALL

This is how Yosemite Valley was formed

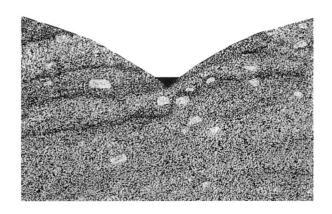

STREAM EROSION. With the uplifting of the Sierra, 25 million years ago, small rock particles in the ancient Merced River began to erode a shallow V-shaped valley in the granite.

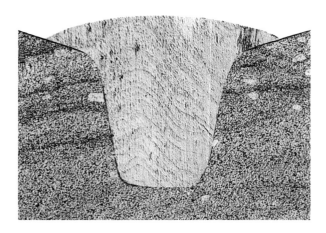

GLACIATION. Beginning with the Ice Age, two million years ago, a series of massive glaciers continued to grind away the rock, eventually changing the valley into a 5000-foot deep U-shaped canyon.

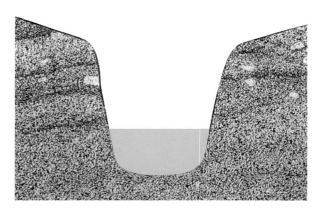

LAKE FORMATION. As the glaciers receded, 10,000 years ago, a dam, or terminal moraine, remained at the lower end of the canyon and a large lake formed behind it. This ancient Lake Yosemite was about 2000 feet deep.

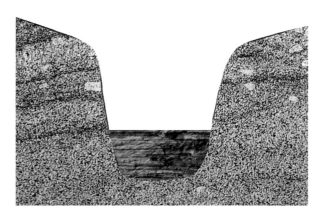

MEADOW SUCCESSION. The lake slowly filled with sediment from the streams, and meadow and forest took root on the level valley floor. This process continues today in all the lakes in Yosemite. Mirror Lake, in Tenaya Canyon, is a good example.

The first people in Yosemite Valley were Native Americans, called the **Ahwahneechee**. They subsisted mainly on acorn meal, hunted with bow and arrow, traded with other tribes, and were skilled basket-makers. Their homes were made of bark, like this one at the Yosemite Museum.

They lived here for about 4000 years before gold was discovered in California in 1848. With the arrival of thousands of miners and settlers, Yosemite Valley was soon discovered and the Ahwahneechee were driven out. Fortunately, no gold was found in Yosemite.

In 1864, in the midst of the Civil War, President Abraham Lincoln signed the **Yosemite Grant** bill, which deeded Yosemite Valley and the Mariposa Grove of Big Trees to California, as the nation's first state park.

But the vast wilderness area adjacent to the Yosemite Grant remained unprotected.

So, in 1890, largely through the efforts of John Muir, Congress passed a bill designating this wilderness area as **Yosemite National Park**, to be administered by the Army.

In 1903, President Theodore Roosevelt visited California and spent several days in Yosemite with John Muir. They visited the Mariposa Grove and camped near Bridalveil Fall in Yosemite Valley.

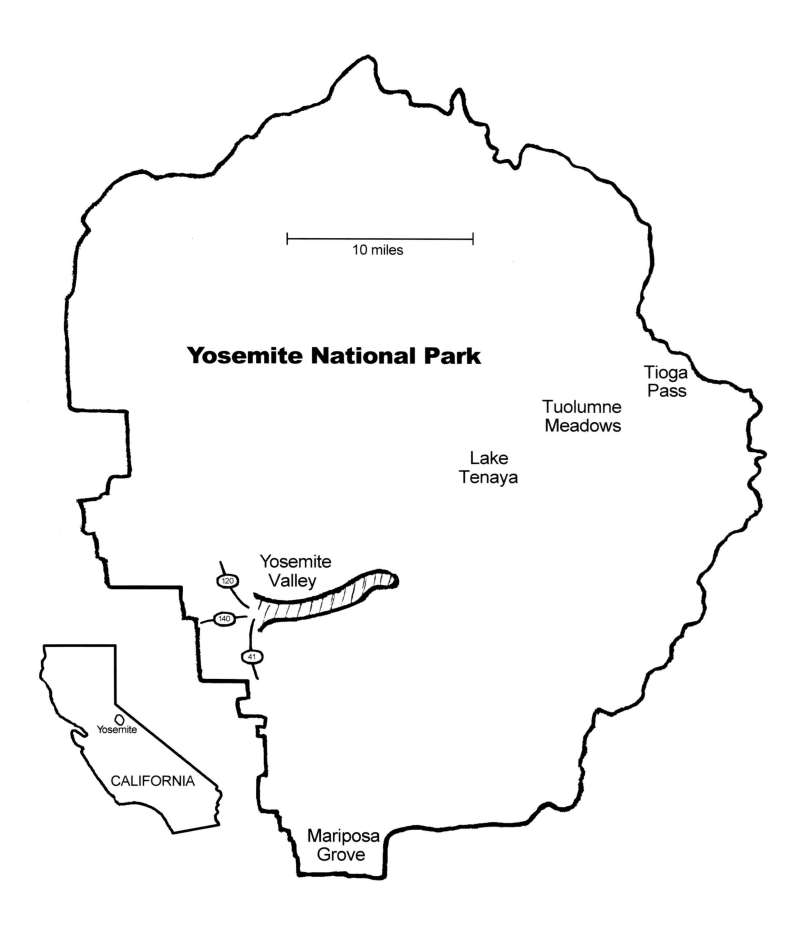

In 1906, the Yosemite Grant reverted to the federal government, and these two parks were combined, under the Department of the Interior, to create **present-day Yosemite National Park.**

Half Dome is the most striking feature in the valley. At an elevation of 8842 feet, its summit towers nearly a mile above the valley floor. ➤

Long ago deep vertical cracks, or joints, caused one side to crumble. Glaciers eventually swept away the loose granite, leaving the sheer northwest face.

The rounded top was formed by exfoliation, rather like an onion shedding its layers. All domes in Yosemite were formed this way.

There are established climbing routes on every dome, spire, and wall in Yosemite Valley. With binoculars you might see climbers on the face of Half Dome.

This is the **back of Half Dome**.

The trail to the top begins at Happy Isles as the John Muir Trail. About three miles beyond Nevada Fall the Half Dome trail branches off to the left and continues behind the dome and around to its far side. It is about 17 miles round-trip and nearly a mile up ... then down.

Hikers use the cable route for the final 400 vertical feet on Half Dome, where it is very steep. ➤

The exfoliation here is impressive.

North Dome, about 3500 feet tall, is just across Tenaya Canyon from Half Dome.

It appears to sit atop **Royal Arches**, with **Washington Column** on the right.

13

The **Ahwahnee Hotel**, a National Historic Landmark, has elegant public rooms and a beautiful dining room. *Ahwahnee* is the Native American name for Yosemite Valley.

Since its opening in 1927, it has been a favorite location for weddings and other special events. Among its many guests have been presidents, celebrities, and royalty.

At **Yosemite Village** you can visit the museum, visitor center, and Ansel Adams Gallery. There is a post office, general store, and several shops and restaurants.

Yosemite Lodge is located near Yosemite Falls and is a pleasant place to stay. There are shops, a bike rental stand, swimming pool, cafeteria, and restaurant.

Deer, raccoons, squirrels, and a variety of birds are seen frequently around the village and the lodge.

The deer in Yosemite are known as mule deer because of their long ears.

According to Indian legend, **Lost Arrow** (upper right) was erected by the spirits in memory of a fearless young hunter, killed here in a rockslide on the day before his wedding.

The top of the spire, at about 3000 feet, is very near the north rim. After an ascent, skilled climbers sometimes slack-line to the rim. Upper Yosemite Fall is at lower left.

This is **Yosemite Creek** as it flows through a hanging valley on the north rim. When it reaches the rim it drops out of sight to become Yosemite Falls.

Hanging valleys result when the main valley is deepened by glaciation, leaving the side valleys suspended. Their streams then become waterfalls.

At 2425 feet, **Yosemite Falls** is the tallest waterfall in North America. It has an upper fall, a lower fall, and a middle cascade which flows in a chasm between the two.

This is the view near the **top of Yosemite Falls**, barely visible at lower left. You are looking down on the **middle cascade** and the trail you took to get here. It is 7 miles round-trip, starting at Camp 4.

Be sure to visit **Lower Yosemite Fall**, an easy 10-minute walk from Yosemite Lodge or the Yosemite Falls bus stop. The fall looks small but actually has a 320-foot drop.

◄ The **Three Brothers** are named for the sons of Tenaya, chief of the Ahwahneechee. The highest Brother, also known as Eagle Peak, is about 3800 feet tall.

Camp 4, a walk-in campground, is the traditional climbers' hang-out. Many now-famous climbers have camped here while planning climbs on Half Dome, El Capitan, or other big walls.

This is a good place to see climbers checking their equipment, bouldering, and slack-lining.

◄ **El Capitan**, 3593 feet from base to summit, is said to be the largest solid mass of exposed granite in the world.

Peregrine falcons nest on its ledges.

There are climbers on this huge monolith much of the year, best seen with binoculars from El Capitan Meadow. The first ascent, in 1958, required several weeks. Most climbs today take one to a few days.

CATHEDRAL
SPIRES

UPPER
CATHEDRAL ROCK

Cathedral Rocks and Spires lie just across from El Capitan

MIDDLE CATHEDRAL ROCK

THE GUNSIGHT

LOWER CATHEDRAL ROCK

The tallest, Upper Cathedral Rock, is about 2600 feet tall.
Bridalveil Fall is on the other side of Lower Cathedral Rock.

Bridalveil Fall cascades from a hanging valley. It appears small but is actually 620 feet tall, as high as two football fields placed end-to-end. ➤

The Gunsight notch is directly above the fall, with Middle Cathedral Rock at upper right.

The Valley Floor Tram Tour is a good way to see the picturesque spots in the valley. The guide is pointing to a coyote in the meadow.

30

Sentinel Rock, on the south side of the valley, stands about 3000 feet high. The Four Mile Trail to Glacier Point starts near its base.

Curry Village, originally known as Camp Curry, was founded in 1899. It has about 200 cabins and over 400 canvas tents, as well as shops, swimming pool, bike rental stand, and cafeteria. The Yosemite Mountaineering School is also located here.

The bears in Yosemite are black bears, though they may be of several colors, and are not dangerous if left alone. They have a keen sense of smell and will break into tents or cars in which they see or smell food. Always store food and coolers in the metal bearboxes.

◄ The **Merced River** meanders through the valley, growing in size as it is joined by Tenaya Creek, Yosemite Creek, and Bridalveil Creek. It originates in the high country from melting snow, and flows over Nevada and Vernal Falls (following pages) before entering the valley.

Rafting is allowed on calm stretches of the river.

Vernal Fall has a drop of 317 feet and is much taller than it appears, as you can see from the size of hikers at the top.

This is a view of Nevada and Vernal Falls from Glacier Point.

The fall is about 1½ miles from Happy Isles by way of the Mist Trail. This trail is very wet in the spring when the Merced River is high.

◄ **Nevada Fall** is upstream from Vernal Fall, and 3¹/₂ miles from the valley. It is 594 feet high.

The John Muir Trail crosses the stream on a bridge just above the fall. Glacier Point is at upper left.

You may see backpackers on the trail, or a mule train taking supplies to Merced Lake High Sierra Camp, several miles upstream.

MORE THINGS TO DO

There are many things to do in the valley. In addition to hiking, biking, and sight-seeing, you can take a ranger-guided tour, ride a mule, camp out, or take a climbing class. You might also take a road trip to Glacier Point.

Ranger-naturalists are very knowledgeable and can tell you anything you want to know about Yosemite, including its history, geology, plants and animals. Sign up for an enjoyable guided nature walk.

Budweiser   Bacardi   Hawkeye   Eeyore

You can take short or long mule rides at the **Valley Stable**, ➤ even an all-day trip to Half Dome. The mules have rather creative names.

Camping is fun, and the summer weather is mild with little rain. Be sure to store your food in the metal bear-boxes to keep it safe.

At the end of the day you can relax in front of the fire with friends and a good book.

Yosemite is one of the best places in the world for rock climbing. The Mountaineering School has **climbing classes** for beginners as well as experienced climbers. ➤

Glacier Point is located on the south rim above Curry Village, and has superb views of the east end of the valley. It's about one hour by car from the valley. Consider taking the bus one-way and hiking down either the Four Mile Trail, or the 8-mile Panorama Trail past Nevada and Vernal Falls.

Summer is the busiest season in Yosemite, but the valley is open year-round. Dogwoods bloom in the spring, when the waterfalls are at their best. In the fall the valley is quiet and the oak leaves turn golden-brown. And in winter the snow-covered domes and peaks are beautiful, with ice skating at Curry Village, and skiing and snowshoeing in the high country.

We have visited only a small part of Yosemite National Park in this introduction, and there are many other spectacular areas.

A one-hour trip to the Mariposa Grove is worthwhile, to see the giant redwoods, many over 2000 years old and with trunks 25 feet across at the base. The drive to the Tioga Pass entrance station, at 10,000 feet and two hours from the valley, is very scenic, with the road skirting Lake Tenaya and Tuolumne Meadows. And with fully 95% of the park designated as wilderness, there are hundreds of miles of trail in the back-country for backpacking.

GOOD-BYE.
COME BACK SOON.

John Muir, when asked by a woman what he would do if he had only one day to spend in Yosemite, replied, "Madam, I would weep!"

૭૭૭૭